T0208485

Who The Lord Is To Me

Who The Lord Is To Me

Tamara Friar

 iUniverse

WHO THE LORD IS TO ME

iUniverse books may be ordered through booksellers or by contacting:

iUniverse
1663 Liberty Drive
Bloomington, IN 47403
www.iuniverse.com
1-800-Authors (1-800-288-4677)

ISBN: 978-1-6632-0047-1 (sc)
ISBN: 978-1-6632-0048-8 (e)

Print information available on the last page.

iUniverse rev. date: 05/13/2020

Contents

Chapter 1

The Lord My Provider

There is nothing in this world that can satisfy. I'm constantly searching for something that will try to quench this thirst that I have. The things in this life: Materialism, acceptance, and popularity can't even gratify. So Who do I look to that can meet my needs of this emptiness that I feel inside? So who do I look to? Who can I go to, who is the One that can fill my cup of this emptiness? Only Jesus, only Jesus, Only Jesus.

Reflection Questions with Scriptures:

Scriptures for Emptiness:

Job 15:32

Job 35:13

Job 35:16

Psalm 95:7-11

Isaiah 55:2

Revelation 3:20

1. Describe a time in your life when you knew that it was only God that provided for you during your circumstances.

_____

_____

_____

_____

2. Are you able to rely on God more now that you have seen him work as a provider? Explain.

_____

_____

_____

_____

3. Describe a time in your life where you felt empty.

_____

_____

_____

_____

Chapter 2

God My Helper

Dear God,

You are my helper. You help me when times get tough. You help me when life is going well. I wait for your response and you're already there, even on unanswered prayer. My helper comes and holds me by my hand, especially when I don't understand. My helper is my first responder that always comes to my aid even when my life seems out of place.

Scriptures and Reflection questions for God's Help

Psalm 46:1-3

Deuteronomy 33:26

2nd Chronicles 14:11

Psalm 10:14

Psalm 27:9

Psalm 37:40

1. Describe a time in your life where you needed God's help.

_____

_____

_____

_____

_____

_____

2. How did he come through?

_____

_____

_____

_____

_____

_____

Chapter 3

God Sovereign Over Circumstances

The circumstances of life seem to never end but I know the One who is in control of them. Part of them comes from our own mistakes, but I know the One who is sovereign enough to give us grace. Yes the grace that none of us can explain. When circumstances come, even I, Tamara should not complain. Why, because the God who knows everything that goes on, everyone must recognize that the sovereign God is in control of them all.

Scriptures and Reflection Questions

Deuteronomy 5:16

Deuteronomy 5:29

Deuteronomy 6:18-19

1st Samuel 2:6

Job 34:21

Psalm 31:14

Psalm 36:9

Psalm 37:5

Proverbs 37:2

1. What does scripture say about trusting God in family life?

    _____

    _____

    _____

2. How can we look at life differently from God's point of view?

    _____

    _____

    _____

3. Give examples of circumstances that we know that we're not in control of?

    _____

    _____

    _____

Chapter 4

God Is My Peace

God is my peace because He knows all of my troubles. When I release the trouble to Him, He brings down true peace. True peace that can only come from giving your life over to Christ. Even when things aren't going well, seek the Lord of Peace who never fails.

Scriptures and Reflection questions for troubles and or trials and peace

2nd Samuel 7:11

1st Chronicles 22:9

Psalm 29:11

Psalm 37:11

Proverbs 1:33

Isaiah 2:4

Isaiah 26:3

Zechariah 13:9

1st Corinthians 10:13

Hebrews 2:18

Hebrews

Reflection Questions for Trouble

1. Where does trouble come from?

    _____

    _____

    _____

    _____

2. How should we respond when we're in trouble?

    _____

    _____

    _____

    _____

3. How does trouble impact our relationship with God?

_____

_____

_____

_____

_____

Reflection Questions for Peace

1. How do believers get peace?

_____

_____

_____

_____

_____

2. Why can't the world experience the peace that believers in Christ can experience?

_____

_____

_____

_____

_____

3. Is it possible to experience peace in the midst of trouble?

_____

_____

_____

_____

_____

Chapter 5

The Strength and Presence of God

You're like a fire that never goes out. You carry me throughout the day. The flame of your presence I cannot contain. The strength of God is also my song. When I'm weak, God is who I call on. He makes me strong. When I walk, Jesus you put strength in my feet in every step that I take. Isaiah 40:31 states, I shall walk and not faint. Lord, I need your strength to speak words pleasing and acceptable to you, because if I don't it's hard for me to follow you. That's why you're my strength, the one which I rely on. Therefore my heart greatly rejoices and with my song I will praise Him-The God of my strength.

Scriptures and Reflections Questions for God's Strength

Numbers 23:22

1st Samuel 2:4

1st Samuel 2:10

2nd Samuel 10:12

2nd Samuel 22:3

2nd Samuel 22:30

Isaiah 40:29-30

Isaiah 45:5

Habakkuk 3:19

Zechariah 10:12

2nd Corinthians 1:21

2nnd Corinthians 12:10

Philippians 4:12-13

1st John 2:14

1. Define strength.

_____

_____

_____

2. How does God supply a believer with strength?

_____

_____

_____

_____

3. Describe some of your weakest moments in your life.

_____

_____

_____

_____

_____

4. Where is God leading you to trust him for strength?

_____

_____

_____

_____

_____

5. Write a prayer for God to strengthen you.

_____

_____

_____

_____

_____

Chapter 6

Lord, Please Ease The Pain

My body remembers this kind of stress that I've had before. Why I pray it away and it comes back, I'll never know. This sickness that I've had. Lord, please bring me comfort which I remember well. You are the God of Comfort even in the midst of pain. The pain that I will go through it's for a reason, even if it's for a temporary season.

Scriptures and reflection questions for healing.

Numbers 21:8-9

Deuteronomy 7:15

2nd Kings 20:5-6

Psalm 41:3

1. Where do you need God's healing provision in your
    life?

    _____

    _____

    _____

    _____

    _____

2. Are you able to trust God's healing power in his
    timing?

    _____

    _____

    _____

    _____

    _____

3. Will you still give God praise even if he does not
    decide to heal?

    _____

    _____

    _____

    _____

    _____

Chapter 7

The Lord Who Makes Me Adequate

So many people in this life say that you're unable to do things because of some limitations that you may bring. I know a God who says that you're capable of handling them. Who is the One that made the limits in you? To show God's glory through you? I'll tell you. My Creator. Just because people say no that's not the end. God prepares you son or daughter for the work at hand.

Scriptures and Reflection Questions For Success

Joshua 1:7

1st Kings kings 2:3

2nd Kings 19:25

2nd Chronicles 20:20

Psalm 28:9

Proverbs 2:1

Amos 5:14

1. In the Bible, there were people that God used for their inadequacies to make them adequate for what God has called them to in their purpose.

_____

_____

_____

_____

_____

_____

2. Where can God turn your inadequacy into a success in your life?

_____

_____

_____

_____

_____

_____

3. What is your success story that God is calling you to overcome?

_____

_____

_____

_____

_____

_____

4. Write a prayer of success that God wants you to achieve in your life.

_____

_____

_____

_____

_____

_____

Printed in the United States
By Bookmasters